# BUILD BRAND
# YO

# BUILD BRAND YOU

## VINCE THOMPSON

MELT Founder, Chairman, and CEO

Award-Winning Brand Builder and Sports Marketer

*Advantage*®

Published by Advantage, Charleston, South Carolina.
Member of Advantage Media Group.

ADVANTAGE is a registered trademark, and the Advantage colophon is a trademark of Advantage Media Group, Inc.

Printed in the United States of America.

10 9 8 7 6 5 4 3 2 1

ISBN: 978-1-64225-195-1
LCCN: 2020918102

This publication is designed to provide accurate and authoritative information in regard to the subject matter covered. It is sold with the understanding that the publisher is not engaged in rendering legal, accounting, or other professional services. If legal advice or other expert assistance is required, the services of a competent professional person should be sought.

Advantage Media Group is proud to be a part of the Tree Neutral® program. Tree Neutral offsets the number of trees consumed in the production and printing of this book by taking proactive steps such as planting trees in direct proportion to the number of trees used to print books. To learn more about Tree Neutral, please visit **www.treeneutral.com**.

Advantage Media Group is a publisher of business, self-improvement, and professional development books and online learning. We help entrepreneurs, business leaders, and professionals share their Stories, Passion, and Knowledge to help others Learn & Grow. Do you have a manuscript or book idea that you would like us to consider for publishing? Please visit **advantagefamily.com** or call **1.866.775.1696**.

*By your own soul, learn to live.*
*If some men force you, take no heed.*
*If some men hate you, have no care.*
*Sing your song, dream your dreams*
*Hope your hopes, and pray your prayers.*
—BO SCHEMBECHLER

This book is dedicated to everyone with a dream. To everyone who has been told no. To everyone who has been told to give up. To everyone who has tasted rejection. Never give up that dream, no matter how big or small; pursue it with zeal, passion, and childlike wonder. I'm still "just a boy from Chatom," and I'm still pursuing my dream every day—and you can too. This book is dedicated to those who will never give up pursuing their dreams. Maybe, just maybe, my story will inspire you to "sing your song and dream your dreams."

# CONTENTS

# WELCOME TO THE REAL WORLD

**If you're like 99.9 percent** of the students who go to college today, you're there hoping for one primary outcome—landing that first job.

The challenge is, they don't do enough in college to teach you *how* to get that job.

I have no doubt you're getting a great education—learning how to reason, how to communicate, and how to analyze information and a ton of important skills you gain studying subjects like history and psychology. But there isn't any class called Getting a Job 101. There's no professor on campus to teach you what you need to know to convince somebody to put their trust in you and pay you to work for them or their company—or at least not many of them.

For some majors, like premed, prelaw, or engineering, typically your career path is mapped out for you, at least at the entry level. But if you're a liberal arts major like I was, once you get your BA, you're pretty much on your own. And that can mean a hard road ahead.

You're probably aware that, particularly in the liberal arts, kids have been coming out of college $100,000, even $200,000, in debt. But at the same time, they're woefully underequipped to build the kind of career success that will help them pay off that debt. And that was before the pandemic. Thanks to COVID-19, if you're in school right now or recently graduated, you're facing the toughest job market in our lifetime. You're going to have a lot of people who have lost their jobs and who, just to get back in the job market, are going to be willing to take a lesser job with less responsibility for less pay than they typically would. It's what people like me call a buyer's market for talent. There are going to be more people in the pool—people with more experience—who are willing to work for less. Meaning

> **If you're in school right now or recently graduated, you're facing the toughest job market in our lifetime.**

these people who already have some real-world experience under their belts are going to be your competition. Plus, there's this whole new world of virtual internships, Zoom interviews, virtual offices … who would have thought it?

That's the reason I wrote this book.

I speak to students at colleges all over the US, and I know some of you are feeling pretty nervous. You're starting your adult life in a crisis. Nobody is sure how this is going to turn out. Well, I call myself the poster child for crisis—I've survived everything from getting fired from my first job, working on a losing political campaign, losing a job with a big company, to starting over, then 9/11 and a recession, and now a pandemic … I mean, pick a subject!

However, through all this turmoil, I've built one of the most successful sports marketing agencies in America.

My company, MELT, specializes in sports, culinary, and other kinds of event marketing, with a focus on college sports events like the Final Four and ESPN College GameDay. I'm also the founder of MELT U, an internship program I started to help students prepare for careers in the sports and event space. I've hired hundreds of people and helped thousands more start their careers, so I know more than a little bit about what it takes to get hired in our industry or an industry like ours.

But that's just part of why I'm writing this. I may be a CEO now, but forty years ago, I was just like you. I was a kid with a passion—in my case for sports and writing about sports—but no earthly idea how to turn four years studying things like history and communications into a job that would pay me actual money to do something that would make me excited to get up in the morning. I had to figure that out on my own. Luckily for me, I also happened to meet the right person in the right place at the right time (more on that later). However, it was still up to me to figure out the rest—how to use my college years not just to get an education, but to develop the habits, make the contacts, and even gain the experience I needed to start my career.

But I did. And if I did it, you can do it too.

**This job market is going to be tough. It's going to be a dogfight.**

Having said that, I don't want to sugarcoat any of this. This job market is going to be tough. It's going to be a dogfight. You're going to get in the tumble cycle sooner or later, so you might as well get ready for it. But I can help. I had to crash through nine million doors in my own career, so I know what works and what doesn't. And I wrote this book to share everything I know about what employers want and what you can do right now to get those doors to open for you, in any job market.

It's all about positioning yourself for that first big job by building your résumé and your network—in other words, you need to "Build Brand YoU," just like the title says.

I promise you, if you follow the advice in this book, at some point you're going to land that job. You're going to land that fish, sink that putt, clear the bases, cross the goal line ... insert sports metaphor here. What I'm saying is, you're going to get that job.

This book will equip you with all the tools you need to do it.

Ready? Then let's do this!

# TAKE THE SHOT

You miss 100% of the
shots you don't take.
**—WAYNE GRETZKY**

**I never expected** to be the CEO of a company that
works with world-famous organizations like Coca-
Cola, Aflac, CBS, Fox, and ESPN. There was nobody
like that where I grew up. My hometown, Chatom,
Alabama, has less than a thousand people and one
stoplight. It's located down in Lower Alabama, just
north of Mobile, Gulf Shores, and Orange Beach.
But to me, it was like growing up in Mayberry (look
up *The Andy Griffith Show* if you don't know what
I'm talking about), and I was Opie Taylor, except my

dad was the mayor instead of the police chief. I spent my days fishing and riding my bike, everybody knew me and looked out for me, and nobody locked their doors. All in all, it was a pretty great childhood.

Still, when I got to Auburn University, I was definitely out of my element. I felt a little like Forrest Gump. Auburn was this big old place with more than eighteen thousand students from all over. All of a sudden, I was surrounded by kids from bigger towns, who had gone to great schools and had seen more of the world. Most of them were older than me too; I didn't even turn eighteen until after I started school. I was overwhelmed to say the least and couldn't find my place. By the way, this is not an abnormal feeling when you go to school. It can be hard to figure out where you fit in. I had a great high school and a great public education growing up, but I could just tell that there was a little bit of a difference between me and my classmates.

I also knew I wasn't getting quite the experience I knew I should be getting at Auburn University. I lived off campus and walked to school. I wasn't meeting people or making a lot of friends; my freshman year was kind of a bust. So I went home for the summer and decided there had to be a different way to do my college experience. I only had four or five years to spend there. I was investing a lot of time, money, energy, and resources. I had a lot of people back home pulling for me to get that degree. So I came back in the fall of 1981 determined to make something different and better out of that experience.

I just didn't know what it was.

What I did know, however, was that I had another advantage. I could just flat-out outwork people. I made a strategic decision to put more effort in, to work harder *and* smarter. Maybe my classmates had some built-in advantages; maybe I couldn't compete with their connections, their money, or their experience, but I had my creativity. And since I knew just being creative wasn't going to be enough to get anyone to pay attention to me long enough to figure out how creative I was, I also decided I was going to have to be *relentless*.

> I had another advantage. I could just flat-out outwork people.

## WHAT DO I MEAN BY "RELENTLESS"?

Being relentless means always looking for an opportunity to be seen, make an impression, and hopefully begin to develop relationships. In my case, it worked like this:

When I started school, my goal was to be a sportswriter. And in my first journalism class, the guest instructor, a man named David Housel, was the faculty editor of the student newspaper, *The Auburn Plainsman*. He also happened to be the head of the school's sports information department.

Being at Auburn in the early '80s was a classic example of being at the right place at the right time, at least from a sports perspective. This journalism class was in the fall of '81, which was also the first year of legendary football coach Pat Dye's tenure. Soon-to-be superstars Charles Barkley and Bo Jackson arrived in '81 and '82, respectively. We also had Olympic sprinter Harvey Glance and Olympic swimmer Rowdy Gaines on campus at that time. We were surrounded by all this crazy greatness—and no internet.

Anyway, I was listening to David Housel, and what he said was mesmerizing to me. All I had thought about was writing, but he talked about all these incredible opportunities on campus just in the sports information department alone. I was like, *Oh my God, I've got to be there right now.* So after the class was over, I worked up the nerve to walk up to him and say, "I want to come volunteer."

Now, he could have said no. But what are the odds somebody turns down free work? He didn't. He said, "Well, get your ass over there this afternoon."

That one encounter changed the whole trajectory of my life. I started working in the sports information department, where I remained for the next three years, while also writing for the *Plainsman*. Housel also convinced me to join Phi Gamma Delta, the fraternity where he was the house father—something I'd had zero interest in because I thought fraternities were just about partying. So I wound up working in sports, getting published, and making the best friends of my life, all because of one guy.

What would have happened had I just packed my bag that day and gone back to my apartment instead of asking that guy if I could volunteer? Would I still be where I am today? I can't say for sure I would be.

**Anybody can be in the right place at the right time if they make it the right place at the right time.**

## GETTING INTO POSITION

That said, as I already mentioned, I get that I was definitely in the right place at the right time. But I'm writing this because, honestly, anybody can be in the right place at the right time if they *make it* the right place at the right time.

Right now, on your campus, there are guest

lecturers scheduled to come talk about all kinds of subjects. There are people working in various jobs like student services or the athletic department or whatever you care about who can be a connection for you and help you start gaining experience. All you have to do is ask. That's what I mean when I say, "Take the shot." You never know where it's going to lead. I definitely never expected meeting David Housel to lead me to where I am, but it did.

## THE ONLY FAILURE IS THE FAILURE TO TRY

Remember, I figured all this stuff out when there was no internet and no cell phones. Your generation has everything you need right in front of you. So if, like me, you're not wealthier or better connected or smarter than your competition, there's still one thing you can control. You can try harder.

I'm not just talking about grades. Of course your major and your GPA are going to be important factors that employers consider. However, they aren't the only factors. The main thing that matters to me is what kind of employee you're going to be—and the best way to get an idea of that is to look at how hard you try.

Look at it this way. If I'm going to invest $30,000, $40,000, $50,000 in you by hiring you to be part of my company, that's coming out of my pocket or the company's coffers. I need to know you're going to be worth the investment, and I'm sorry to say, a high GPA doesn't really tell me that. What if you spent all that time hiding in the library? Employers are looking for problem solvers, people who are getting out there, meeting people, and sometimes getting their knees scraped.

> **Employers are looking for problem solvers, people who are getting out there, meeting people, and sometimes getting their knees scraped.**

Remember, the competition in this post-COVID job market is going to be brutal. You may feel like you've been through it already since you got into college and that was competitive, but this is a whole different ball game. With college, you were applying to be one of thousands. Applying for a job, you are thousands of one.

But look at it this way. This is going to be a journey. You're probably not going to have some huge overnight success—but that's okay, as long as you have a focus and a goal. And you have to accept that you're probably going to get thrown off that goal sometimes. You're going to get thrown off that saddle. The important thing is to keep getting back on and trying again and taking every shot you see—and then going the extra mile in everything you do.

If you do that and follow the steps I lay out in this book, you're going to set yourself apart from most of those thousands of people you're competing with and get into the top fifth percentile. And if you keep being relentless and keep building Brand YoU, at some point you're going to land the job.

So where and how can you start building that brand? We'll cover that in the next chapter.

# COLLEGE IS THE ULTIMATE PROFESSIONAL LAB

The difference between who
you are and who you want
to be is what you do.
—BILL PHILLIPS

**When you think of college,** you probably picture
big old buildings and crowded classrooms, football
games and frat parties. You probably don't picture a
massive career lab or professional center packed with
hidden opportunities to gain real-world experience in
just about anything you want to do. But it's there on
your campus right now. You've already got the tools

to start building almost any career you want.

Then again, what if you don't know what career you want?

I say, "Do what you love, and the money will follow."

Growing up, I had a passion for sports. I wasn't very good at playing sports, but I loved to watch different sports (and I was very good at watching). I also loved to write about sports. I'd write stories for my local newspaper and letters to my heroes and those types of things. So I started college planning to be a sportswriter. It sounded like a no-brainer.

When I met David Housel that day in my Intro to Journalism class, I learned that there were all these other opportunities to work in sports just within the Auburn athletic department—some that would put me right on the sidelines with the players. And those very same opportunities probably exist on your campus right now—and not just for liberal arts majors like I was. Let me explain.

Assume that at a major university, the athletic department is roughly a $100 million organization. Within that organization, there are dozens of different areas where you can gain real-world experience no matter what your major is. Just look at the ticket office. The ticket office drives a ton of revenue in an athletic department. They sell tickets to football games and basketball games and women's softball games and on and on. So there are skills you can gain there if you're pursuing a degree in business or accounting or even math. It's also a great place for students who are interested in data analytics—you can use your time in the ticket office to examine who your season ticket buyers are—when they graduated, their backgrounds, their household incomes, the cars they drive, the beverages they drink, how much money they donate to the university, and more. Multiply that by forty or fifty or sixty thousand season ticket holders, and suddenly working in the ticket office is a giant opportunity.

Then there's content and video. There are so many opportunities there, from pulling cables to jobs like writing and editing. The sports teams themselves need content created and video crews to record the games. There are also organizations like the SEC Network filming and streaming (and marketing and advertising) all these games in some platform or format. So that's another bucket. And of course, there's also social media—you can work with the athletic department to help the teams and athletes reach their audience or even start your own social media business and work with athletes directly (once they can generate revenue when the laws change in 2021).

Then there's a separate department that does nothing but put the events on. You don't think about all the moving parts involved when you walk into a football stadium or softball stadium or a volleyball court or a basketball court. There's a whole group of people making sure whatever the event is, it flows well. They're overseeing the concessions, the ticket takers, the security, the restrooms, the ingress and egress, and more. Meaning this is a place to get very valuable event management and venue experience. There are obviously hundreds of events going on every year, just in sports.

Then there are the day-to-day operations of the athletic department. If you've got a $100 million organization, there are a lot of moving parts. That is probably why I can confidently tell you I've never heard of an instance where a kid went to an athletic department and wanted to volunteer and got denied. There's just too much to do.

There are even opportunities in sports for psych majors. The mental health area is growing, probably because there's so much anxiety out there. So, if you're studying to be a mental health professional and you like working with athletes, there may be an opportunity for you in that area of the athletic department. Or, if you're an education major or enjoy helping people understand, say, chemistry or physics or English lit, you can volunteer (or even get paid) to tutor athletes. Or if you're into health and fitness, you can help with athletes' nutrition or conditioning.

In other words, in sports alone there are more opportunities than you can possibly imagine. In case I've missed any, there's also

- NIL (name, image, likeness);

- brand development;

- rules compliance;

- fan-alytics;

- eSports;

- and more.

That's how, instead of just writing about sports, I was able to become part of the *world* of sports. Just because I was able to recognize these opportunities and take advantage of them. And I built relationships through them. Maybe I started out driving Dick Vitale to the airport and showing Paul Finebaum around campus, but those people, and dozens of others I met in college, have been part of my career

**The people you meet right now, in college, could be helping to shape your career for years to come.**

and my life for nearly forty years.

Meaning the people you meet right now, in college, could be helping to shape your career for years to come. You just have to figure out where they are.

## FINDING OPPORTUNITIES THROUGH YOUR PASSION

Of course, sports are my passion, but your passion may be something completely different. The only thing that matters is that it's *your* passion, not someone else's idea of what you should care about. The idea is to start doing it as soon and as often as you can.

Whatever your area of interest might be, your first goal should be to figure out where the opportunities are in that area. Because I promise you, you're never going to be in an environment of opportunity equal to what you're in right now. I used sports as an example, but there are events happening on campus every day. For instance, on an average major college campus, there are two hundred to three hundred separate donor and fundraising and development officers. Whatever your passion is—if it's Greek life, if it's student government, if it's a club—your goal is to put yourself in that environment by volunteering or reaching out to people, getting involved, and taking the shot.

Some places to try include

- the alumni department, where you can meet and network with all the prominent alumni of your school;

- the career development office, where you can pitch in and help with career fairs and other networking activities;

- your specific school or college—for example, the College of Liberal Arts;

- food services and campus hotels, which offer great ways to work and learn on the front lines of the hospitality industry;

- campus health, fitness, recreation, and intramural departments, where you'll find great ways to learn operations, organization, and the fitness industry;

- student services for events like fun runs, concerts, festivals, guest speakers, and more;

- campus-based service organizations;

- political organizations; and

- causes and community organizations.

I want to take a moment to talk about causes,

since so many young people seem to be involved in them. Whatever cause you care about, whether it's feeding the hungry or animal rights, there's probably an opportunity to get involved right on campus. Most fraternities and sororities are affiliated with a cause, and many national and international nonprofits have branches on campus.

If you're interested in media, you probably have access to a campus radio station, a campus television station, the campus newspaper, the website and social media department, and on and on. Whatever your area of interest, the goal is to find a way to get yourself into that environment and volunteer. No matter what you wind up doing, you're networking, you're learning, and you're building your résumé. Which, together, helps to Build Brand YoU.

But what if, even with all this information, you can't find an opportunity to do what you want to do on campus? Don't let it stop you from getting experience and building a portfolio. You can be a talk show host right now, just using your computer and inviting campus influencers to chat. There are online platforms where you can post your art, your writing, or even your

**Whatever you want to do, the key is to stop thinking about it and find a way to do it.**

own movies. Whatever you want to do, the key is to stop thinking about it and find a way to do it. The more you do, the more your portfolio—of tangible work and of skills and life experience—grows.

## GETTING NOTICED

Once you figure out where the right opportunities are, your next step is to do whatever you can to get to know the people and gain experience in your area of choice. That means getting up in front of them and volunteering your services, like I did with David Housel. But before you do, it's best to be prepared. Have some business cards printed up with your name and contact information, so you leave them with a great impression of your professionalism and preparedness. Give those cards to everyone you meet.

When the job starts, be sure to interact with the people you work with. You want to form relationships, so even if you're shy, find a way to connect. Strive for excellence in whatever you do, whether it's making phone calls or pulling cables—remember, it's only as important as you make it. And when you're finished, send the gatekeepers (like the receptionist at the front desk) and any other important people involved a handwritten note saying, "Thank you for the opportunity. Next time you're back on campus (or need help with something), I'd love the opportunity to do it again."

This is how you start to build not only a portfolio of work, but a network of people in the field you want to work in. In addition, by taking these opportunities, meeting these people, and opening yourself up to these experiences, you are actually taking the first steps toward building Brand YoU. We'll take a closer look at the nuts and bolts of subject in the next chapter.

# YOU ARE YOUR BRAND

Determine who you are and what
your brand is, and what you're not.
The rest of it is just a lot of noise.
**—GEOFFREY ZAKARIAN**

**Students today are a lot savvier than I was.**
When I graduated from Auburn University in 1984, I had written probably two hundred articles that were published and produced hundreds of events. I didn't do that well in school other than my journalism classes, but I had this monster portfolio full of evidence that I was the guy you could count on to give it 110 percent. I even gave myself a nickname: VinnyInc. Actually, my fraternity brother (and now

Auburn mayor) Ron Anders, who will kill me if I don't give him credit, came up with it. But I liked it enough to keep it. It fit me. I wasn't in college to waste time. I was there to take care of business.

Still, through all that, I never realized that while I was working and networking and adding to my portfolio, I was also building "Brand Me."

I guess that's because back then we didn't think of people as being brands, the way Coca-Cola and Nike are brands. Now, with social media dominating the way we communicate, your generation sees it differently. But you still might not be aware of how to develop and control your own personal brand and how to position your brand to put you in that 5 percent of applicants who rise above the rest. You want your brand to put you in the position to win. We'll tackle how you do that in this chapter.

## DISCOVERING BRAND YOU

Everything you do while you're in school, everything we talked about in the last chapter, contributes to your brand—whether you know it or not. It's the face everyone sees (and the qualities everyone thinks of) when they think of you. And yes, by everyone, I mean potential employers and internship coordinators.

You're just starting this process. You're beginning the relationship-building process. You're beginning the follow-up process. You're beginning the networking process. You're beginning the audition process. Because that's really what it is, every time you make a new connection. It's an audition. You are showing that person who you are. When you build Brand YoU, the idea is to show yourself in the best possible light.

> **You have total and complete control over the face you show the world.**

The good news is you have total and complete control over the face you show the world. It's all in how you position and present it. That's the essence of branding.

You might not be entirely clear on what your brand says about you yet, and that's okay. Because right now, I'm going to help you figure that out *and* shape your brand so it shows you in the best possible light—laser focusing on the qualities you want people to see (and leaving out those you'd rather they don't see). One simple way to do that is to create a *brand board* or, as I like to call it, a *professional destination board.* A brand board is like a vision board, where you put a bunch of words and images together to give you an idea of what matters to you. It works like this:

1. Search for words and images that resonate with your passion. Copy or cut out the things that reflect your values, your ideas, your goals, and your experiences.

2. Next, look through all the images you've selected. Keep the ones that resonate the most with you, and get rid of those that don't. Make a Pinterest page that is about you specifically.

3. Download these images, and build yourself a vision board so you can see them every day.

4. Look at your finished product, and ask yourself what it says about you. What matters to you? What do you care about? What are your values? That's Brand YoU.

5. Over time, make any adjustments you need to make. Feel free to remove and add things to reflect your brand as it develops.

## TELLING YOUR BRAND STORY

The way you package and present yourself determines what *brand story* you tell. But what's a brand story?

Whatever you've done with your time in

school—whether you ran a danceathon, produced a fun run, were heavily involved in your fraternity or sorority, were independent and part of a club, or were a barista—the way it will be perceived is all packaging and positioning. That's easy if you were president of your sorority or editor of the paper. Titles send clear information about you that makes it easy to stand out. But what if you spent most of your free time working to put yourself through school? That's when you focus on the *story* of what you did at work. How you developed relationships with your regular customers, perfected your knack for problem-solving, or juggled logistics ... you get the idea. It's not about the title; it's about the effort and effect. And honestly, even if you were president of your sorority, if you don't talk about the results you achieved in the position, it's meaningless to me. The effort you make is what tells me if it's worth investing in you. You want to show signs that you're a self-starter. Show signs that you have initiative. Show that you have that willpower to keep building that résumé, to make that effort to network, to put yourself in the environments where you can keep gaining experience.

Of course, everything you do helps to shape Brand YoU—not just those things you decide to put on a vision board. That includes your relationships and connections, so choose your friends and activities carefully. Who you are seen with is part of the face you present to the world. So are the things you're seen doing, which brings me to the next subject.

## BRAND MANAGEMENT

Once you establish a brand, you have to make sure you reflect the values of that brand in everything you do. This is called brand management. It's knowing what fits with Brand YoU and what doesn't fit—what people in our business call "off brand"—and then eliminating it. And the best way

**Define your values and live by them.**

to start narrowing that down is really pretty simple: just define your values and live by them.

Now, don't freak out about that. I'm not saying you can't have fun in college; Lord knows I did. But I was lucky. I went through college before the internet, before everybody's permanent record was on social media for everyone to see. Now, your social media accounts are the first place potential employers are going to look for information about you. Let me rephrase that: your social footprint is the *first thing* we look at!

And that can be a problem. I see kids doing

really stupid stuff on Snapchat, Instagram Stories, and TikTok, and I think, "There is no way I'm ever going to hire you. Ever." You don't want that to happen to you, and there's no reason why it should. Remember, *you control your brand.* So my advice is, whatever you post online, make sure it passes the "grandma test." Meaning, if you wouldn't feel comfortable showing it to your grandmother, keep it in a private photo album and off social media. Or better yet, don't do the thing that gets the picture or video taken in the first place. I'm not saying don't express yourself, but the point here is to *showcase* yourself.

There are much better things you should be doing with social media anyway. We'll get to those in the next chapter, when we explore LinkedIn.

# GET LINKEDIN!

Things turn out best for the people who make the best of the way things turn out.

**—JOHN WOODEN**

**You're probably on** Snapchat, TikTok, and Instagram. Maybe you're on Twitter or Facebook too. But are you on LinkedIn? Probably not.

But you should be.

LinkedIn is quite simply the greatest professional networking tool ever invented. Why? Because *everyone* in business uses it. I'm on LinkedIn. The head of ESPN is on LinkedIn. Any professional person in your field who you might want to meet is probably on LinkedIn too. And if you're on LinkedIn, you have a much better chance of making that meeting happen. That's what the platform is actually designed to do—"link" people in the business world together.

Look at it this way. Back in the old days, I had to haul out the Yellow Pages (ask your parents what that is) or go to the library and look this kind of information up in the encyclopedia or some resource guide. You guys have it at your fingertips. There's no excuse for you to not be able to find almost any information you need—and LinkedIn is the perfect place to start.

## HOW TO BUILD A LINKEDIN PAGE

Before you can get started meeting people through LinkedIn, you have to create a LinkedIn profile where they can find you and communicate with you. So what should you put on yours? Here's a quick guide through the process.

### Step 1: Explore

Before you build your own profile, take some time to explore the LinkedIn profiles of some leaders you admire. Notice how they describe themselves and talk about what they do. Also take some time to look at the profiles of younger people you know, maybe people who were a year or so ahead of you in school. Their pages will be closer to what your page will look like, since, like you, they're at the beginning of their careers.

### Step 2: Summarize

Once you've seen enough pages to have a feel for them, you can start writing your own summary page showcasing Brand YoU. In a brief and concise manner, describe who you think you are and what you are looking for ... but do it in a way that subtly highlights any initiative you've taken and what you've accomplished in your life. For example:

> *I'm a former high school and college lacrosse player and leader in the student government at Auburn. Seeking to connect with people who share my interest in sports marketing.*

Of course, it doesn't have to be sports related; it can be government or music or whatever your interest is. The point is to come up with a clear and concise description of who you are and why you're there.

### Step 3: Smile!

You'll notice there's a spot for a photo. Make sure you upload a professional photograph—no candid shots, no family photos, no party pics. Remember, this is a business tool, and you want to be taken seriously.

## Step 4: Showcase

Don't stress too much over your résumé. No one is going to expect to see years of high-level experience on the résumé of a college student. Remember what we went over in the last chapter about how to build Brand YoU. It's all about packaging and presentation. Even if you were a barista at a Starbucks, for example, your story is what matters. Instead of saying you were a "barista" or "server," you might say, "I was on the front lines of customer service, managing hundreds of transactions per day." Showcase the skills you learned, how hard you tried, and the impact you had. Remember that every employer is looking for self-starting, self-initiative, and discipline. This is your first pass at that communication. Demonstrating those things will put you ahead of the pack, including that sorority president who thought she could get by on her title.

> **Remember that every employer is looking for self-starting, self-initiative, and discipline.**

## Step 5: Participate

That said, if you get into filling out your LinkedIn profile and discover you don't have anything to put in there, you've got larger problems, because that means you're sitting in your dorm room playing video games. Go back to chapter one and then get out into the world and do something—then come back. Build that brand and pad that résumé!

### Step 6: Repurpose

The good news about doing all this work, just for a social media profile? You may be starting the process on LinkedIn, but you can use updated versions of the same material in all your job and internship applications. This is a tool that will be with you for the long haul.

One other note: if you can possibly afford it, I highly recommend getting the premium version of LinkedIn, because it gives you a lot of advantages that you can really use during a job search. For example, LinkedIn Premium allows you to see who's looking at your profile, which then gives you the ability to plumb all their connections. You can send messages to people's in-boxes and message them more easily. In the past, LinkedIn has offered free-for-a-year deals for students, but if that isn't the case and you can't afford the fee, a standard LinkedIn profile will work just fine. Because the real power comes from how you use LinkedIn as a targeting tool.

## USING YOUR LINKEDIN ACCOUNT

The whole point of LinkedIn is to connect with other people—and in your case, you want to target those people in your field you most want to meet. Make a list of them before you start and use the search feature to find them. Their profiles should contain all the information you need to reach out to them in a meaningful way.

The way you reach out on LinkedIn is, ideally, the same way you will reach out when you're looking for jobs and internships. All that personal info you can see in a person's LinkedIn profile can be used to tailor your message to them. Look for an emotional connection—for example, if you're in the same field or went to the same school or have a friend or acquaintance in common. Whatever you can leverage, use it to stand out from the crowd of people who want this person's time and attention.

**Never send your résumé with your first message to somebody.**

One important reminder: Never send your résumé with your first message to somebody. Don't forget to "soften the target" first. Just keep it simple.

For example, if I get a message that says, "Hey, Mr. Thompson, I notice you're an Auburn grad. I'm a junior at Auburn too." Or a message that says, "Hey

Mr. Thompson, I'm studying marketing. I see you've been very successful in sports marketing. Do you mind if I use you to reach out to other people within your LinkedIn community?" I'm going to respond to that message because that person tried. They were polite; they did their homework; they learned something about me. Why wouldn't I take a minute to respond to them?

In fact, I take it as a measure of pride to respond to everybody that reaches out to me. But that doesn't mean everyone you will encounter will react the same way. Keep in mind that these are busy people you're trying to reach, and they may even test your ability to "be relentless" by forcing you to reach out a few times before they respond. Don't take it personally. Just keep pushing forward. Remember that all these efforts are, in effect, an "audition" or a series of tests designed to showcase what kind of employee you will make.

We'll learn more about how to build that showcase for Brand YoU in the next chapter, where we will explore how to create a résumé.

# THINK OF YOUR RÉSUMÉ AS A BLIND DATE

I don't believe in miracles.
I believe in character.

**—PAT DYE**

**Your résumé is going to be** your first introduction to a potential employer or internship coordinator. They don't know you from Adam, as if someone set you up on a blind date. So, when you go on a blind date, what do you do to get a second date? It's all about chemistry. It's about finding a way to form that connection with somebody so they want to get to know you better. I call it the Great Woo. It's about showing just enough of who you are, in just the right light, so that you pique the person's interest and land that coveted second date—or in this case, a job or an internship.

If you're going to do that with a résumé, you've got to put it together in a way that makes it clear exactly why a person should want to interview you. And that all comes back to packaging and presentation.

*You* are your résumé, not just the piece of paper that lists a bunch of jobs and internships and volunteering and extracurriculars. You want your résumé to be a picture of you as an employee, not a just list of stuff you've done. That means writing your résumé to tell the story of Brand YoU we talked about in chapter 3.

**My approach to a résumé is to focus on you as a person as opposed to a list of stuff you've done.**

## HOW TO WRITE A RÉSUMÉ

Regardless of what format you use, my approach to a résumé is to focus on you as a person, as opposed to a list of stuff you've done. It uses what's called an **inverted pyramid format**, with your brand story at the top and all the details, like jobs and grades and GPA, at the bottom. The goal is to paint a picture of who you are as a potential employee (or intern or even volunteer) and what they can expect from you. Remember, nobody is going to expect a kid just out of college to have years and years of work experience, and your grades don't really tell the story of what kind of employee you'll be, so don't sweat that stuff too much. What matters most is the wooing—getting the reader interested in you as a person and imagining you as an employee. Once you light that spark, the details don't really matter.

Here's how you do it.

## Inverted Pyramid Format

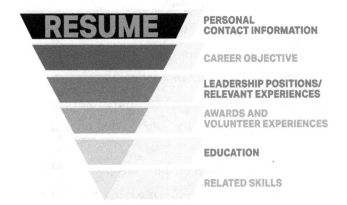

RESUME

PERSONAL CONTACT INFORMATION

CAREER OBJECTIVE

LEADERSHIP POSITIONS/ RELEVANT EXPERIENCES

AWARDS AND VOLUNTEER EXPERIENCES

EDUCATION

RELATED SKILLS

## Step 1: Define Your Career Objective, or Your Positioning Statement

Start out by explaining, in one or two sentences, what you're looking for, both long term (the career part) and short term (the actual position you're applying for). You want to link the two and show why the job you're applying for matters in terms of your life goals. For example: "My objective is to be the head of social media for a major sports organization, and I'm looking for any opportunity to get my foot in the door and gain experience." If you have any major accomplishments that are relevant or indicate that you're a self-starter—if you were an Eagle Scout or class president, for example—you will want to work them in. After all, they're part of Brand YoU. Customize this part of your résumé as you approach different firms and different people, because employers want to know how you are going to bring value to *their* organization.

## Step 2: About Me

This is where the wooing, meaning most of your thinking and writing, comes in. Basically, this is where you tell your brand story and lay out the details of why you will make such an awesome employee. This is the most important part of the résumé, because it's where you get to show growth by explaining *what you've learned* from your experiences. Demonstrating that you've been awake and learning paints the picture that says, "This is why you need to be investing in me."

Just because it's important, that doesn't mean you need to overthink it. Just start by saying something like, "The reason I'd make a great employee is because …" and then tell your story. "I've put the effort behind my grades." "I volunteered for the sports information center." "I worked on the fundraising campaign." Don't forget to include outcomes, like, "I ran a fundraiser that raised $15,000 for juvenile diabetes." You can include outstanding high school achievements—things like all-academic, student government, or anything that stands out—just remember to continue the story through college and show how you've built on those skills. For example: "I was student-body president in high school and am currently vice president of my fraternity." You want them to be able to see that growth path.

And remember, if you've been working full time to put yourself through school and haven't done anything exciting, like hold a major office or coordinate some massive event, you still have a brand story. You still have the skills you developed on the job, the problems you solved for your employer and/or customers, how you managed to balance work with school. It's just packaging and positioning to show them how hard you're willing to work for what you want.

Employers really do take that seriously. At least I do. One time, a young lady approached me at Auburn and told me she was working three jobs while maintaining a 3.0 GPA. Sure, that was out of 4.0, but three jobs? I was like, "Are you kidding me?" That's the kind of hustle I like to see. This woman had me at hello! Then she said, "I don't really know if I'm going to be in sports, but can you help guide me into cause-related marketing?" And I told her, "Well, yeah, I know the people at the Arthritis Foundation and Boys and Girls Club and Cerebral Palsy and Habitat for Humanity and on and on and on. I'll introduce you to all of them."

And I did. And that was it.

The point is, just because your experience isn't high level, or even directly related to the field you want to work in, doesn't mean it doesn't matter. Again, it's as important as you make it.

### Step 3: List Your Professional, Volunteer, and Extracurricular Activities

Here's where you get to list everything you've done, job by job—the area traditionally referred to as "work experience." Again, don't worry about how much actual experience you have. List all your jobs and activities, paid and unpaid, but make sure you don't just give a list of bullet points of what you did. Make sure to list outcomes, achievements, and results. That's what employers want to see.

### Step 4: Finish Up with the Basic Details

Include your school, major/degree and graduation date, GPA, and other information.

### Step 5: Make It Pretty!

Check your spelling and grammar to make sure everything looks and reads professionally. View your résumé on your phone to make sure it's clear and easy to read. Bold any key words that make you stand out, so readers get the full picture of what Brand YoU is all about.

## MAKING SURE YOUR RÉSUMÉ GETS READ

To put it simply, don't apply to generic websites, and don't send out a generic pitch!

You don't want to put all that work into a résumé only to have it end up in the recycle bin. But that's what's likely to happen when you send a résumé in cold, through a job website or through an email to "jobs@" or "info@" a company. When that happens, you have to get past the bots—the applicant tracking system (or ATS) that automatically filters out some résumés and sends them to the trash without a single human ever seeing them. There are some basic tips to avoid this, like "focus on skills not goals" or "use key words" or "pay attention to formatting and spelling." But there's no reason to ever need them in the first place.

If you want to make sure your résumé gets read, don't send it to the bots in the first place. Send it to a *human*. Here's how:

### Step 1: Soften Your Target

Identify the hiring manager, the CEO, or whoever the gatekeeper might be. Search for their email address or, better yet, find them on LinkedIn, which is the easiest sight line to help you figure out who the gatekeepers and/or decision makers are. Or better yet, ask the people you've met through your college activities or the people at your school who are involved in your field for information and even

> **Do whatever you can to learn about the person who will be receiving your résumé *before* you submit it.**

an introduction. The point is to do whatever you can to learn about the person who will be receiving your résumé *before* you submit it.

### Step 2. Hit Your Target

I'm ambivalent as to whether it's better to send an email or a hard copy of your résumé, but either way, the next step is finding the exact way to find the target. That means you want to send your email or hard copy directly to a human. Not hiringmanager@melt, not info@melt, not careers@melt. Once you know who you want to target, it's not that difficult to find their email or physical address.

If you send an email, you need a subject line. Obviously you want to keep the person reading, so incorporate a piece of the info you've uncovered to make a connection and keep them from deleting it. Something like "Fellow Auburn student interested in cause marketing." Then add a brief note that elaborates on those connections and tells a little about you. "Hey, congrats on your success. I'm a current Auburn student, and I volunteered for Habitat for Humanity and coordinated this year's fundraiser. Would you please consider my résumé for advice or potential employment?" That way, you set your request up as an inoffensive gesture, *inviting* the person to consider you.

Bottom line—what employers want to know is how are you going to bring value to their organization if they're going to invest their time, money, and resources in you. You want your résumé to display to that employer how you would be as a future employee. This is the best way I know to put together and send out a résumé that will paint that picture and get you past the blind date stage and on to that second date.

Now we'll take a look at the first place you will be using that résumé—taking Brand YoU out for a test drive by applying for internships.

# ALL ABOUT INTERNSHIPS ... OR, ER, VIRTUAL INTERNSHIPS

Champions keep playing
until they get it right.
**—BILLIE JEAN KING**

**Do internships matter? Hell, yeah, they do!**
Of course, as the guy behind MELT U, one of the most successful college internship programs in the sports and event industry, I'm a little biased. In fact, all our entry-level employees are graduates of MELT University. It's company policy.

And since you're reading this book, I'm assuming that by this point, you understand that the way you spend your time during your college years is going to determine how employers see you later. They'll be looking at your résumé for skills, experience, and growth, and there's no better place to gain them than an internship or virtual internship.

Competing for an internship is like a trial run for the job search you'll be doing after you graduate. It's still going to be a giant numbers game, only not quite as epic, since you're still in school and probably still living with Mom and/or Dad, so this isn't "real life" yet. But an internship search is about as close as you can get to what entering the job market is going to be like. There could be dozens, hundreds, or even thousands of kids competing against you for just a handful of spots, or even one spot, depending on the size of the company and the program. So you need to get serious about landing an internship for next summer right now, even if you're a freshman. You need to be relentless—and also strategic.

**You need to be relentless—and also strategic.**

By strategic, I mean there are things you need to do in advance to beat out those dozens or hundreds or thousands of other kids. Getting an internship is a twofold process—there's the preparation you do while you're in school, building Brand YoU and padding your résumé, and then there's actually getting out there and pursuing the internship. We've already covered the first part, so this chapter will focus on the second.

# HOW TO SCORE AN INTERNSHIP

### Step 1. Start Early!

When I say early, I mean *now*. The internships you're applying for may not start until next summer, but you need to start the application process no later than right after Christmas. At MELT U, we start getting inquiries in the fall for the next summer. When you start late, you send the message that you really don't care that much. And you know where that's going to lead … straight to the recycle bin.

### Step 2. Do Your Research

Before you start filling out applications, find out as much as you possibly can about the companies you're targeting and their internship processes, especially now that many may be virtual. There's nothing to prevent you from starting that today. Go on LinkedIn and Google, and learn whatever you can about the companies you want to work with and the gatekeepers who are in charge of their internship programs. This information will help you later.

### Step 3. Leverage Your Connections
### and Relationships

Have you met anyone through your campus activities who is involved with a company you want to intern with? Let them know. Even if you don't know anyone who's directly involved, be open with everyone you work with about companies you'd like to intern (or work) for. You never know who knows whom and who can give you the personal introduction that will put you ahead of the pack.

### Step 4. Make It Personal

Every once in a while, I'll get some inquiry that says, "Hey, I was just wondering if your company offered internships." To which I reply, "Have you been living in a cave for the past ten years?" Well, I don't actually reply, but I think it … as I hit the delete button. Which is what I do with the forty thousand other inquiries I get that are addressed to info@meltatl or that start with the words, "Attached is my résumé and cover letter."

If you want someone like me to care enough to read your application, take the time to show you actually care about the company. Use the information you gathered through your research to tell the person why you want to work for their organization. Let them know how excited you are about the opportunity and why you're a great candidate. For example: "I want to be in sports marketing. I've researched the top sports marketing agencies in America. You're one of those I've heard about, because you spoke at my school, and I'd like to be a part of the intern program." That sets you apart from everyone else who didn't take the time to make that connection.

**If you want someone like me to care enough to read your application, take the time to show you actually care about the company.**

### Step 5. Don't Apply Blind!

Again, if at all possible, track down people's addresses so you can send your application directly to a decision maker. If it's not possible and you have to use the generic site, make your brand story as appealing as possible on the application itself. And even if you ultimately wind up having to submit your résumé through a generic site, you can still make the effort to track down and reach out to the people involved directly. If you can't find the email, type up a nice letter, attach your résumé to it, and snail mail it. Although not being able to do something as simple as tracking down a person's email might be a red flag … you'd have to be living in a cave to not find mine!

### 6. Follow Up!

If you really, really want to land an internship, follow up. Drop the coordinator or the CEO or whomever you've been communicating with a brief, polite email or note saying something like, "Hey, Mr. Thompson, thanks so much for considering my internship application. I'm really excited about the prospect of working with MELT—hoping to hear from you soon."

So, what can doing all this work to land an internship get you? Let me tell you about one student I worked with recently. She came in to interview for a spot at MELT U very polished, very buttoned up. She made eye contact; she was prepared; she knew all about this organization and all about me. So I said, "Hey, we want you in the program, and if you complete the program, complete the requirements, really show us what you got, you'll move into a full-time role here." And she did. We spent four years in the trenches together producing major-league meetings with The Coca-Cola Company, ESPN's College GameDay, the NCAA Final Four, and many, many others. And she was such a superstar that The Coca-Cola Company called me one day (and they'd never done this before) and said, "We'd like to bring her over." And I said, "Wow, that's a very, very flattering, very high compliment that somebody who has been within my organization has impressed you enough that you want her to go to work for Coca-Cola." And today, that onetime intern is a rising star at The Coca-Cola Company.

In other words, her brand was 100 percent on point! And as we move into this new world of virtual internships and Zoom job interviews, the same set of rules she followed still applies, whether you're trying to land an internship or a job. (Note: some of these topics will be expanded on in the next chapter.)

- Bring the heat.

- Dress professionally.

- Do your research—know your target and everything you can about the organization and the position you're applying for.

- Have a concise brand story.

- Look them in the eye.

- Interview the interviewer.

- Put your phone where you can't see or hear it (to avoid distractions and losing eye contact).

- Have a professional backdrop (for virtual interviews).

- Ask about next steps, thank them for their time, and ask how to follow up.

- WRITE (do not email or text) a personal, handwritten note.

- Win!

If you give it your all, an internship can not only help build Brand YoU but take you right into your first job ... and beyond. We'll take a closer look at how to apply for that job in the next chapter.

---

# BE RELENTLESS (THE JOB HUNT)

You can't get a job without experience and you can't get experience until you have a job. Once you solve that problem you are home free.

**—JACK BUCK**

**Yeah, I know,** I've already talked about being relentless in this book. But if there's one time when relentlessness is more important than at any other time, it's when you're trying to land that first job. Because, if I haven't made it clear by now, it's going to be tough. Job hunting was already a numbers game before COVID—I've always said you've got to make a hundred casts to get eight bites to land two fish. You might need to double the number of casts now. In other words, you have to be prepared for a lot of rejection. Remember, it isn't personal. It's just the way it goes. We're all in the "rejection business," so keep moving!

But you can still give yourself a huge advantage and put yourself in that top 5 percent of applicants by being prepared. You've already done the work to get here. Now you need to prepare yourself for the reality that all that work might not lead to your "dream job." Especially in this market, you might have to do whatever you can just to get your foot in the door. That may mean taking something that's beneath what you expect or think you should be doing.

But I promise you, it's worth it just to begin getting that experience and getting some money coming in. Your first job doesn't have to be your dream job. Mine certainly wasn't. It's what you do with the job once you get it that matters.

Now, that doesn't mean I'm saying to just go out there and apply for any random job in any business, at least not right off the bat. In a job market this crazy, that may ultimately be necessary, and if it is, that's okay. You can still use that time to focus on building whatever skills you can, solving problems, and, most importantly, putting in effort. You're still using the time to build Brand YoU by gaining real-world experience, no matter what you're doing.

However, at least until you've exhausted every other possibility, focus on the jobs that will get you as close as possible to the kind of environment you ultimately want to be working in and/or the kind of work you ultimately want to be doing. You'll make more of the kind of contacts and get seen by more of the people who can help you down the line. Basically, it makes the trip to where you want to be shorter, and you can look to establish relationships with mentors who are willing to help advise and guide you along the way.

It's kind of like volunteering to pull cables as a way to get involved in ESPN College GameDay. You want to do whatever you can to put yourself in an environment where you can showcase your brand by demonstrating what a great employee you are and how happy you are to be there to the people who can help you move forward. Any job that can help you do that is a *great* first job, no matter what the title or salary might be.

## WHERE TO FIND THOSE JOBS

Just as you do with internships, you may already have a target list of companies you're interested in working for. That's a great place to start, because I can almost guarantee there are more companies connected to your area of interest than you even know exist. Which brings us back to LinkedIn. Get on and look up the people and companies you're interested in and check out their contacts. See who's affiliated with them, and spend some time researching what they do. The idea is to get as clear a picture as you can of the field you want to work in and all the possible "ways in."

**The idea is to get as clear a picture as you can of the field you want to work in and all the possible "ways in."**

At some point, you're also going to need to get off your computer or your phone and actually talk to people. Now is the time to reach out to all those contacts you've made through your college career and take them out for coffee (if that's safe in your area, of course). And yes, some of those people will be busy and may prefer to help you over email or phone or Zoom, if they help at all. But the more relentless you are, the more people you reach out to, the better your chances of finding a way into a company you'd love to work for. That's why it's important to pursue and cultivate mentors. They will be invaluable in your life's journey.

So make an effort to reach out to everyone you know in one form or another. Tell them you're graduating and entering the job market; ask for their suggestions, their recommendations, and, most importantly, their introductions. When you see people in person, bring your business cards, which makes remembering you easy for them and also looks impressive. And to make sure you're remembered, send everyone you reach out to a handwritten note thanking them for their help. It's not only polite; it's also another opportunity to remind them of your existence and general awesomeness.

If you put in the effort, you should wind up with a substantial target list of people to contact at companies where you're interested in working. Which means it's time to send out your résumé.

## HOW TO SUBMIT A RÉSUMÉ

Since you've read this far, I'm going to guess you already know what *not* to do when sending out a résumé. That alone is going to help you stand out. Even today, with your generation being social media savvy and knowing so much about personal branding,

I can't tell you how many submissions I get that start out, "Attached please find my résumé and cover letter for the position of accounting coordinator. My starting salary is $35,000." What am I, as an employer, going to make of that? Why would I want to hire that person? What's in it for me? The same thing happens when I get a résumé addressed to info@meltatl. You've got a better chance of getting hit by lightning than of getting a job with that.

Applying for a job is a *process*, not an *application*. And a large part of that process is getting your résumé

**Applying for a job is a *process*, not an *application*.**

into the right hands and making the right impression. So, again, take the time to learn something about the person you're sending your résumé to. Reach out to them on LinkedIn if you can, or send them an email with a subject line that will get their attention. For example, say in your subject line that you know someone in common or that you went to the same school or that you've been preparing for a career in their field.

Also—explain why you want the job! As an employer, I'd much rather hire a person who's excited about the job than someone who just wants a paycheck. Explaining why you want a job is part of demonstrating why you're the best person to do it. For example: "Dear Mr. Thompson, I hope you're managing well in the crisis. Congratulations on your success. I see a job posting for account coordinator. Here's why I believe that I would be a great account coordinator (because of X, Y, and Z). And I'm willing to come in there and work my fingers off from day one."

Finally, you also want to remove as many barriers to opening your résumé or any attachments as you can. If I've got to jump through seven hoops to open your portfolio or it's difficult to look at for any reason, I'm probably going to jump ship. It's like driving by a billboard on the interstate. You're going to get about ten seconds of my time, so make it short, quick, simple, and sweet. But also make sure that the quality of the work you're sending represents the best quality of the work that you've done.

And once you've sent your résumé, follow up! Email the person you sent your résumé to and ask for an appointment with them or HR or whoever talks to potential employees. Connect with the person you're trying to reach on LinkedIn, and then maybe follow up with an email saying, "Hey, I sent you a résumé …" Again, remember it's a numbers game. You've now hit this person three times. You've made the effort to reach out in writing. You've made the effort to reach out on LinkedIn. You've made the effort to reach out via email. You're building that cadence of communication to open that door.

That's what I mean when I say be relentless. The job market is going to be tough. You're going to need to put in maximum effort, and that means hitting people multiple times in order to get a response. But hey, I do the exact same thing. I'm very successful in closing business transactions, but rarely do I close them on the first phone call. It may take days, weeks, and even months or years sometimes.

So just stay relentless. That's how you get someone like me to call you in for an interview. We'll take a look at what to do when you get there in the next chapter.

# BRING THE HEAT! (THE JOB INTERVIEW)

You never get a second chance
to make a first impression.

**—OSCAR WILDE (OR WILL ROGERS)**

**You're almost across the finish line.** You've rounded the corner and landed the interview. This is your chance to close the deal and make the move from your college career to your actual career. The last thing you want to do is blow it now. No pressure, right?

Interviewing for your first job is stressful. But if you're prepared going in and you follow a few simple tips, it can be a lot easier. Especially if you know exactly what people like me are looking for (and what drives us nuts) when we interview a candidate for a job. So here is everything you need to know to make the best first impression possible.

## STEP 1. DO YOUR HOMEWORK

If I haven't hammered this point home enough by now, I'll say it one more time. You should know everything you can possibly know about the company you're interviewing at and the person you're interviewing with going in.

## STEP 2. COME PREPARED

Unless you're told otherwise, as we used to say in the country, come dressed in your "Sunday best." Your clothes should be neat, clean, and pressed, and they should be professional. So bust out that iron or spring for the fluff and fold. Make sure you bring your portfolio with you, along with several copies of your résumé.

## STEP 3. BE POLITE.

It should go without saying, but a job interview is a time to be on your best behavior—with everyone. I've seen people destroy what was otherwise a perfectly fine interview by not being nice to the person at the front desk or to my assistant. Displaying that kind of attitude is a red flag no employer is going to ignore. At least I know I'm not.

On that note, and this is the most important point I'm going to make in this entire chapter …

## STEP 4. TURN OFF YOUR ****ING PHONE!

Seriously. The moment you are called in to interview, shut your phone off and put it away. Do not set it to vibrate. Do not look at it. Do not even touch it. This is a cardinal sin. It's amazing how many people do it!

## STEP 5. WIN THE INTERVIEW

When you meet the person who will be interviewing you, immediately look them in the eye and say "Hey" or "Hello" or whatever is most natural for you. Your goal is to connect with this person, to get them to see why they should hire you. This is where all that research you did comes into play. Use it to demonstrate your knowledge of the company and how much you want to work there, or if you're talking to the CEO, focus on the person you're talking to and their accomplishments. You can also bring up people or things you have in common or scan the office for things to spark a conversation—you can see where the interviewer went to school, if they have a family or a dog, what their hobbies are. This is what I mean by "interviewing the interviewer." The point is to make that connection so you can demonstrate that you're engaged, you're interested, and you're serious about the position and the company. That will get the person doing the interview to take you seriously.

**One sure way to ace an interview with me is to get me talking about myself.**

One sure way to ace an interview with me is to get me talking about myself. My line is, "Enough about me. Let's talk about me some more." But I use the very same tactics when I pitch a new prospect. I don't make it about me; I make it about them. Yes, even I "interview the interviewer." I'll be in a meeting and say something like, "I looked you up on LinkedIn, and I see you've had this giant career in the hotel business. Tell me how you're handling the commute from New York to Atlanta and how you manage your family?"

This is the same thing I did thirty-five years ago, when I was just starting out. About a year after I graduated, I had an opportunity to apply at a PR firm. I really, really needed this job. So I researched the founder; I researched the agency; I researched his clients. I probably knew more about that company than the guy who interviewed me.

As a side note, I also went (and at the time it cost a lot of money to do this) and made a printed copy of my portfolio of two hundred articles to leave behind. I wanted them to have physical evidence that I was capable of writing a press release when they were sitting around talking about me versus other candidates. If you have a portfolio of work, you might want to make a similar investment.

Because the end of the story is, I got the job. And that turned out to be the job that launched my career.

## STEP 6. BE FLEXIBLE!

Sometimes I'll meet with a candidate and decide on the spot that I want to introduce them to some other members of my team. I'll say something like, "Hey, I like you. Do you have some time to go see three of my top account people?"

Would you believe I have actually had people respond, "Well, no, I've got to go."

Are you kidding me? You worked all this way to get to the CEO, and he's telling you that you're going to have a chance to go talk to some other people that can influence the hiring process? And you "got to go"?

That's just one example. But if you reach a point in an interview where the person you're talking to likes you enough to introduce you to another person, don't be an idiot … SAY YES!

## STEP 7. GET REFERRALS

Interviewing for a job isn't always about that particular job—it's also a major opportunity for networking.

> **Interviewing for a job isn't always about that particular job—it's also a major opportunity for networking.**

Every person you meet helps build Brand YoU by adding to your network of professional contacts, especially after you do your research and impress them during the interview. So when you're wrapping up, especially if you've been told there are no opportunities, say something like, "Now that we've met, would you mind giving me a couple of names that I could contact?" And presto, you have two or three more people to contact who might wind up giving you a job.

# STEP 8. FOLLOW UP

I like to say that if you want to make it in the new school, you have to go back to the old school. That means, after your interview, always send a handwritten (not emailed!) note to each person you met with, thanking them for their time. Most people don't, so it's impressive and makes you stand out right off the bat.

If you don't hear back right away, let it gestate for about two weeks. Then give the company a polite nudge. If you've made a connection with the front desk person or the gatekeeper, start with them, or go straight to the person who interviewed you and send a follow-up email that says, "Hey, Mr. Thompson, just following up. Is there anything right now? Or do you know any other people I could connect with? If not, I'll check back with you in another month or so." You're being respectful of the person's time, but at the same time, you're letting them know you're still interested and that you don't give up easily.

Finally, look for an opportunity to volunteer. Add something to your note like, "By the way, I noticed you're doing the Final Four in Atlanta. Is there an opportunity for me to come out and volunteer? I'll do whatever you need me to do."

Who could turn down an offer like that? I

wouldn't, and chances are, neither will the person you interviewed with. Just keep being relentless, and eventually, you're going to get the job.

# KEEP THE JOB YOU GET

I've missed more than 9,000 shots in my career. I've lost almost 300 games. Twenty-six times, I've been trusted to take the game winning shot and missed. I've failed over and over and over again in my life. And that is why I succeed.

**—MICHAEL JORDAN**

**Looking back over the trajectory of my career,** I think if there's a secret to my success, it's that I wasn't afraid to get my knees skinned. I got roughed up a lot out there. I still do. But I stayed relentless, because being relentless is part of *my* brand. I never gave up, and I have a career I couldn't have imagined in my wildest dreams.

But underneath it all, I'm no different than you. I'm in the same business you're in, just at a different level. I'm getting told no ninety-nine times a day, just like you.

> I never gave up, and I have a career I couldn't have imagined in my wildest dreams.

Except maybe I'm different in one area. Maybe because I never knew how far it would take me, I was willing to work my butt off from day one. But not everyone is. And I've got to tell you, as an employer it kind of infuriates me when I see kids who aren't willing to pay the price the way I was. I'm not pretentious about my success. I still answer my own phone. I still return my own emails. I still put my trash outside the door. I don't ever ask anybody in my organization to do anything that I'm not willing to do. So when somebody tells me they're not willing to do something, let's just say it doesn't bode well for their future with the organization.

Which is sad, actually. You'd think after doing all that work to land their first job, a person would want to keep it.

Then there are those kids who, within six months after starting their first job, come to me and want to know their "career path." To which I reply, "Your career path is getting your ass hit on that glass door on the way out!" I just have no tolerance for this behavior.

Bottom line: there isn't a perfect job. Unless you make it the perfect job. Unless you get in there and give 110 percent every day and take every opportunity you can to meet people and learn things and grow your network and build your portfolio. That's how you find your perfect job. And even better, it's how you keep it.

> **Bottom line: there isn't a perfect job. Unless you make it the perfect job.**

I always say you can't rob the castle until you get the keys to the front door. That's when you get in, and then you start nibbling around the edges and picking the pockets and raiding the rooms. And then all of a sudden, you've got a million-dollar account.

Put the work in now, and the rewards will follow. And you won't just find your dream job—you'll build your dream career and Build Brand YoU into an unstoppable force in any job market.

# ACKNOWLEDGMENTS

**This book would not be possible** without the support of thousands of people whom I have crossed paths with in my life—way too many to acknowledge here, but you know who you are, and maybe we'll get around to you in the next book (or maybe not), but here is a try:

To my son, Carter, my True North, everything I do I do for you.

To my parents, Maudeen and Jack, for always letting me dream my dream and doing everything in your power to always support my dream.

To my "modern family": Gwen, Stefhan, Chelsea, and Cecil.

To Holly, well, just for being Holly.

To those who've always believed in me: Bryan Hubbard, Trey Endt, and Mayor Ron Anders (who dubbed me "VinnyInc").

To the amazing MELT team for being the

greatest team on earth and for all of your support in this process.

To my publishing partner Advantage and to my ghostwriter, Lisa Canfield—one word: "Amazing"!

To all the great folks in my hometown of Chatom, Alabama, or, as we say, "God's Country." And to Washington County High School for my amazing education.

To all the great people at Auburn University, for all the opportunities that great university gave me.

To David Housel, even though I think he fired me at least six times!

To those who fired me from my first job (you know who you are).

To Barry Huey, who gave me my first real professional shot.

To Richard Scrushy, who gave me a real view of the real world.

To The Coca-Cola Company, for being my first client and for twenty years never stopping believing in me. There are too many names to name, but Jim Dinkins, John Mount, Dina Gerson, Kasia Horner, Katie Bayne, and David Preston, to name a few, were my early believers and still are!

And lastly to the Good Lord from whom all blessings flow, for answered (and some unanswered) prayers.

# RECOGNITION FOR
# VINCE THOMPSON AND MELT

 2020 - **Atlanta Magazine Top 500:** *Vince Thompson*

 2019 - **ABA Company of the Year: Marketing, Advertising & PR** - *Melt*

 2019 - **Summit Award - Social Media Campaign: ESPN College GameDay Snapchat** - *The Coca-Cola® Company*

 2019 - **BIZBASH Top 1,000:** *Vince Thompson*

 2019 - **Cynopsis Sports Media - Best Use of Snapchat: ESPN College GameDay** - *The Coca-Cola® Company*

 2019 - **Interactive Marketing Influencer Campaign of the Year Melt/Valser Influencer Strategy and ATL Launch** - *Valser*

 2019 - **Atlanta Magazine Top 500:** *Vince Thompson*

 2019 - **Chief Marketer 200, The Top Marketing Agencies:** *Melt*

 2018 - **Event Marketer's Top 100 "IT" List** - *Melt*
- **Best Pop-Up Retail Experience:** *The Coca-Cola® Kitchen*

 2018 - **Cynopsis Social Good: Melt University** - *Melt*

 2018 - **The Drum Marketing Awards, Best Event/ Experiential Strategy - Finalist: AVID Hotels Pop-Up Tour** - *IHG*

# RECOGNITION FOR
# VINCE THOMPSON AND MELT, CONTINUED

 2018 - **BIZBASH Top 500 Most Influential:** *Vince Thompson*

 2018 - **PR News Social Media: Best Use of Filter:**
ESPN College GameDay Snapchat - *The Coca-Cola® Company*

 2018 - **The Shorty Awards, Best of Social Media:**
ESPN College GameDay Snapchat - *The Coca-Cola® Company*

 2018 - **SBJ Power Player: College Sports -** *Vince Thompson*

 2018 - **ABC Most Admired CEO:** *Vince Thompson*

 2018 - **ABA Brand Experience of the Year:** *The Coca-Cola® Kitchen*

 2017 - **Multi-Brand Shopper Solution:**
**Taste of the Tournament, -** *The Coca-Cola® Company*

 2017 - **ABA Agency of the Year:** *Melt*

 2015 - **ADA Father of The Year:** *Vince Thompson*

 2015 - **Wellspring HOPE Award:** *Vince Thompson*